2850

lake

Nurse

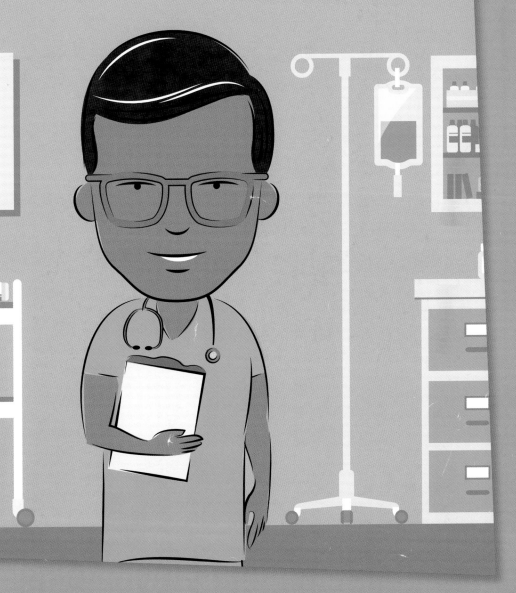

Published in the United States of America by Cherry Lake Publishing
Ann Arbor, Michigan
www.cherrylakepublishing.com

Reading Adviser: Marla Conn MS, Ed., Literacy specialist, Read-Ability, Inc.
Book Design: Jennifer Wahi
Illustrator: Jeff Bane

Photo Credits:
© Oksana Kuzmina / Shutterstock.com, 5; © Spotmatik Ltd / Shutterstock.com, 7; © Michael C. Gray / Shutterstock.com, 9; © Africa Studio / Shutterstock.com, 11; © Diego Cervo / Shutterstock.com, 13; © Olesia Bilkei / Shutterstock.com, 15; © XiXinXing / Shutterstock.com, 17; © Monkey Business Images / Shutterstock.com, 19, 21; © ESB Professional / Shutterstock.com, 23; © aleksandr-mansurov-ru, 2-3, 24; Cover, 1, 6, 14, 18, Jeff Bane

Library of Congress Cataloging-in-Publication Data

Names: Bell, Samantha, author. | Bane, Jeff, 1957- illustrator.
Title: Nurse / Samantha Bell ; [illustrated by Jeff Bane].
Description: Ann Arbor, Michigan : Cherry Lake Publishing, [2017] | Series:
   My friendly neighborhood | Audience: K to grade 3.
Identifiers: LCCN 2016056589| ISBN 9781634728317 (hardcover) | ISBN
   9781634729208 (pdf) | ISBN 9781534100091 (pbk.) | ISBN 9781534100985
   (hosted ebook)
Subjects: LCSH: Nurses--Juvenile literature.
Classification: LCC RT61.5 .B45 2017 | DDC 610.73--dc23
LC record available at https://lccn.loc.gov/2016056589

Printed in the United States of America
Corporate Graphics

About the author: Samantha Bell has written and illustrated over 60 books for children. She lives in South Carolina with her family and pets. She is very thankful for the helpers in her community.

About the illustrator: Jeff Bane and his two business partners own a studio along the American River in Folsom, California, home of the 1849 Gold Rush. When Jeff's not sketching or illustrating for clients, he's either swimming or kayaking in the river to relax.

Nurses help us get well.
They take care of us.

Nurses work with doctors. They both help us when we are sick.

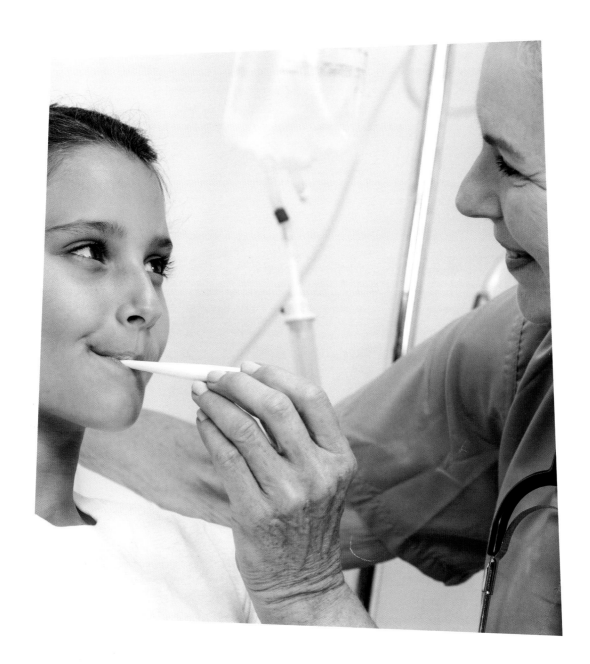

Some nurses work in schools.
They help sick students.

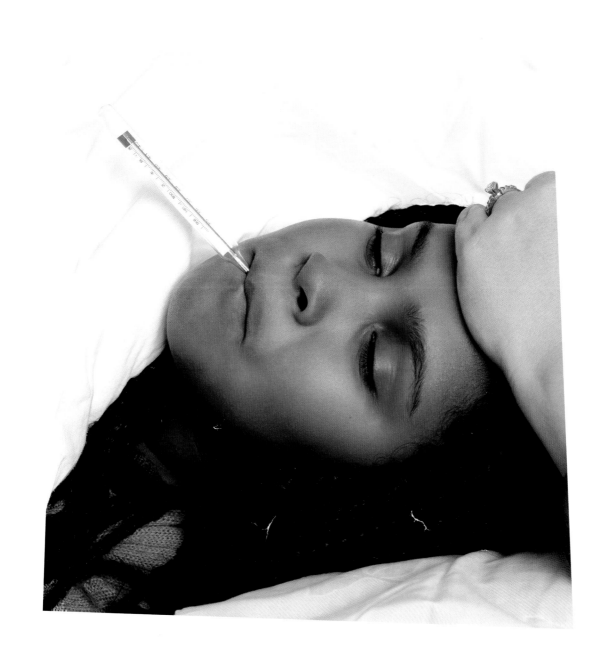

Some nurses check their eyes. They make sure students can see well.

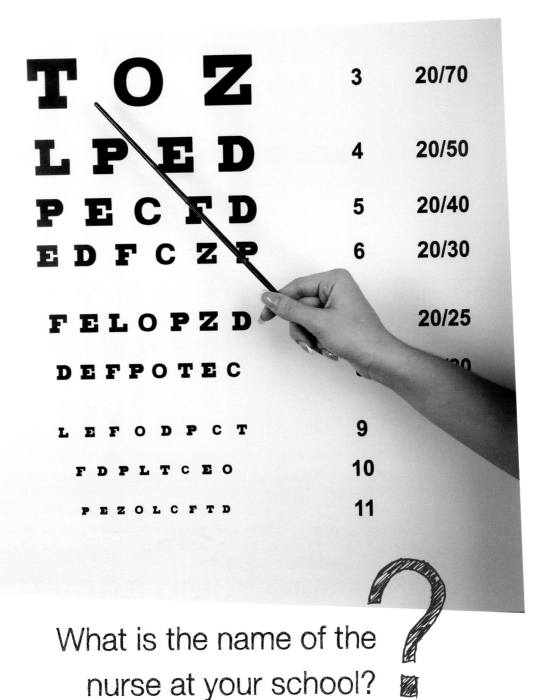

What is the name of the nurse at your school?

Some work in **nursing homes**.
They take care of older people.

Some work in hospitals. Some help new mothers. Some help new babies.

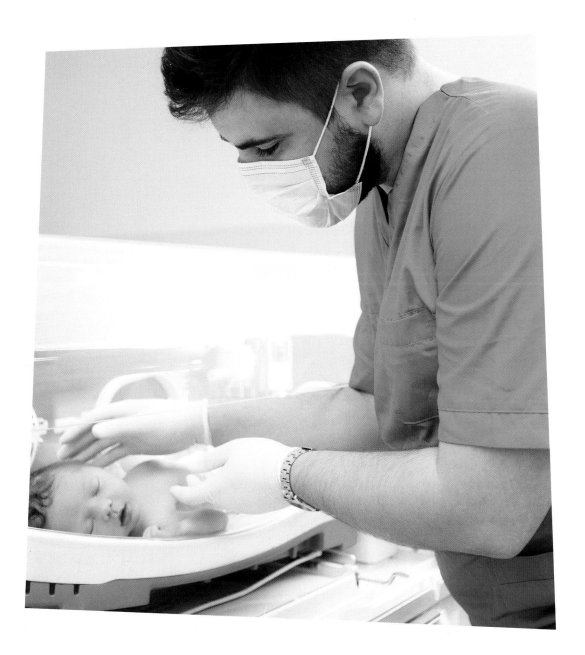

Doctors talk to **patients**. They explain things to them. Nurses make sure patients understand.

Where have you seen a nurse?

Sometimes people stay in the hospital. Nurses check on them. They bring them what they need.

Nurses listen to the patients.

It is hard to be sick. It is hard for families, too. Nurses help **comfort** them.

What would you like to ask a nurse?

glossary

comfort (KUHM-furt) to make someone feel less pain or worry

nursing homes (NURS-ing HOHMZ) places that offer full-time care to disabled or elderly people

patients (PAY-shuhnts) people who are getting treatment from a doctor

index

+

E BELL

Bell, Samantha.
Nurse.
Central BEGINRD
03/18

DISCARD